NINE-WEEK STUDY GUIDE

SEVEN
WORDS
—— *you* ——
NEVER WANT
TO HEAR

ISBN 978-1-64645-775-5 (paperback)
ISBN 978-1-64645-777-9 (ebook)

Library of Congress Control Number: 2022923192

NINE-WEEK STUDY GUIDE

SEVEN WORDS *you* NEVER WANT TO HEAR

How to Be Sure You Won't

DENISE WILSON

REDEMPTION PRESS

CONTENTS

ACKNOWLEDGMENTS

Had it not been for the encouragement of Robert Pratt, this study guide may never have come to be. I have never met Robert but became acquainted with him after he wrote to me via the contact form on my website. In his letter, he expressed a desire to see group study materials available that would go along with *Seven Words You Never Want to Hear*. At **88**, Robert is still involved in prison ministry and has sent my book to several inmates. Although we haven't met in person, I consider him a dear brother in Christ and am so grateful for his encouragement.

It was not my original intent to write a companion study so I want to thank each person who encouraged me in that direction and helped me persevere.

Thanks to my friends, Donna Sutherland and Sonia Cochrane, who each gathered a group to read and discuss *Seven Words You Never Want to Hear* using the questions at the end of each chapter. Their experiences inspired me even further to complete this study guide.

Never-ending thanks to my mother who read over each draft of this study and offered feedback along with constant encouragement.

My husband, Brad, continues to support and encourage me. I am truly blessed to have a husband who loves me in so many practical ways.

Thanks to Gino Geraci for taking the time to discuss the tests of genuine faith with me and offering feedback on the seven tests found at the end of this book.

When the study guide was close to completion I was blessed to have an amazing team come alongside me and offer feedback. Thanks to Laura Armstrong, Amy Glendinning, Sarah Poling, Loretta Tolly and William Scheremet. Each offered valuable thoughts that have made this study better than it ever would have been without them.

A special thanks to Donna Chapman whose friendship, guidance, and encouragement has gone over and above what I could have hoped.

I also want to thank my editors Inger Logelin and Judy Hagey for their patience, guidance, and help.

Thanks to everyone who encouraged me and believed in me and in the importance of this message.

Finally, I thank the Lord who saved me, and gave me a passion for sharing the gospel.

To God be the glory.

A NOTE FROM DENISE

When life is over and you stand before God, what will he say to you? Wouldn't you like to have the answer to that question?

Some genuine believers lack assurance of salvation, while others believe themselves to be Christians when, in fact, they aren't. Some doing this study will be genuine believers, and self-examination will affirm that. Others may think they are truly born again but, through the process of self-examination, may discover that they are not.

God *wants* us to have assurance (1 John 5:13). He *warns* us not to be deceived (1 Cor. 6:9–10).

The way to know whether a profession of faith is genuine is by self-examination. That's why Paul exhorts those in the Corinthian church to examine themselves.

> Examine yourselves, to see whether you are in the faith. Test yourselves. Or do you not realize this about yourselves, that Jesus Christ is in you?—unless indeed you fail to meet the test. (2 Cor. 13:5)

My prayer for you as you work through this study of *Seven Words You Never Want to Hear* is that you will be given insight into your standing with God. This will be a time for self-evaluation under the penetrating light of God's Word.

A false hope cannot save, but a sure hope will give you assurance and draw you even closer to God.

HOW THE STUDY WILL WORK

You have likely heard the question, "How do you eat an elephant?" If so, you know the answer is, "One bite at a time." The good news about this study is that the bites are small. It takes just fifteen minutes a day, five days a week. In nine weeks you will have completely read *Seven Words You Never Want to Hear* and studied important biblical passages that go along with the message.

This workbook is useful for both individual and group study, but if you do this study with a group, you may find the truth more penetrating as you interact with others in stimulating discussions.

Through many years of participating in Bible studies, I have come to realize the daily work in a study is just as important as the weekly group time. When you get into God's Word on your own, the Holy Spirit is your teacher and the time can be rich.

None of us wants to hear the words, "I never knew you, depart from me." This study will show you how *to be sure you won't.*

What do you say? Are you in? You won't regret it . . . there's a lot at stake.

Denise Wilson

Short video testimonies and a leader's guide
are available at denisewilson.ca.

WEEK ONE

I can't think of anything worse than going through your entire life thinking you are a Christian, only to find out at death you are not.

The sobering passage we will study this week shows this will be the reality of "many" who claim to know the Lord.

> Not everyone who says to me, "Lord, Lord," will enter the kingdom of heaven, but the one who does the will of my Father who is in heaven. On that day many will say to me, "Lord, Lord, did we not prophesy in your name, and cast out demons in your name, and do many mighty works in your name?" And then will I declare to them, "I never knew you; depart from me, you workers of lawlessness."
>
> —Matthew 7:21–23

DAY 1

Read the Introduction of Seven Words (pages 1–2).

The above passage is part of the Sermon on the Mount found in Matthew 5–7. That sermon begins with the Beatitudes which describe those who belong to the kingdom of heaven.

1. Read Matthew 5:2–11 and list the characteristics of those who belong to the kingdom of heaven.

v. 3 _____ _Poor in spirit_ _____

v. 4 _____ (Read 2 Cor. 7:10 for clarification)

v. 5 _____

v. 6 _____

v. 7 _____

v. 8 _____

v. 9 _____

v. 10 _____

> Examine yourselves, to see whether you are in the faith. Test yourselves. Or do you not realize this about yourselves, that Jesus Christ is in you?—unless indeed you fail to meet the test!
>
> —2 Corinthians 13:5

Charles Spurgeon was a passionate Christ-centered preacher. Yet, in a sermon using 2 Corinthians 13:5 as a text, Spurgeon acknowledged his own need for self-examination and his desire that his listeners also examine their hearts.

One of the prayers I often pray, and desire to pray as long as I live, is this: "Lord, let me know the worst of my case. If I have been living in a false comfort, Lord, rend it away; let me know just what I am and where I am, and rather let me think too harshly of my condition before thee than think too securely, and so be ruined by presumption." May that be a prayer of each heart, and be heard in heaven![2]

examine

(verb)

To inspect closely.
To test the condition of.
To inquire into carefully: INVESTIGATE.[1]

Self-examination can serve two purposes. It can bring assurance of salvation to the true believer, or it can cause doubt and healthy concern for the false convert.

2. Write out David's prayer in Psalm 139:23–24.

*3. Take a moment to talk to God. You could use the prayer of Spurgeon or David as a guide.

*Throughout the study, you will see questions with an asterisk. These are personal questions, not to be taken up during the Group Study time. Feel free to answer them openly and honestly, knowing they are not being shared.

DAY 2

Read Chapter 1, "The Christian Home Syndrome" (pages 3–9).

1. What elements of a prayer to accept Christ do you think are essential?

*2. What evidence in your life points to being transformed into a new creation? Consider 2 Corinthians 5:17: "If anyone is in Christ, he is a new creation. The old has passed away; the new has come."

3. Is how a person lives an indicator of true salvation? If so, why?

DAYS 3 and 4

Read Chapter 2, "How Jesus Evangelized" (pages 11–22).

*1. What areas of your lifestyle would Jesus be likely to challenge?

*2. When confronted about sin in your life, how do you respond? Are you willing to turn from it as the Samaritan woman did, or are you like those from the region of the Gadarenes who sent Jesus away?

*3. What are some things in your life that don't conform to Jesus' standards but are hard for you to forsake?

*4. What is a religious deed that you are tempted to put your faith in?

*5. The rich young ruler was unwilling to give up his possessions. Is there anything in your life that you struggle to give up for Jesus?

DAY 5

1. Whose righteousness must you exceed to enter the kingdom of heaven (Matt. 5:20)?

2. What kind of righteousness did the scribes and Pharisees have (Matt. 15:7–9)?

3. Who will enter the kingdom of heaven (Matt. 7:21)?

4. Who will not enter the kingdom of heaven (Matt. 7:21–23)?

5. Identify the contrasts found in Matthew 7:13–14.

Two gates	_____	_____
Two roads	_____	_____
Two destinies	_____	_____
Two groups	_____	_____

6. List the characteristics of those who are known by God.

Read the following passages to assist in your answer: John 10:27–28; 1 Corinthians 8:3; John 10:14; 2 Timothy 2:19.

*SELF-EXAMINATION

Reflect on what you have read, studied, and learned in this week's lesson and record what your self-examination has revealed to you about your salvation. Record your answers.

Assurance :

Doubt :

Concern :

"

The call to careful self-examination receives its urgency from the very great danger there is of self-deception. Sin darkens the understanding, so that man is unable to perceive his real state before God. Satan "hath blinded the minds of them which believe not" (2 Cor. 4:4). The deep-rooted pride of our hearts makes us think the best of ourselves, so that if a question is raised in our hearts, we are ever prone to give ourselves the benefit of the doubt. A spirit of sloth possesses us by nature, so that we are unwilling to go to the trouble that real self-examination calls for. Hence, the vast majority of religious professors remain with a head knowledge of the truth with outward attention to forms and ceremonies or resting on a mere consent to the letter of some verse like John 3:16, refusing to "make their calling and election sure" (2 Pet. 1:10).

—A.W. Pink[3]

GROUP STUDY QUESTIONS

many *(adj)* consisting of or amounting to a large but indefinite number.[4]	**few** *(adj)* consisting of or amounting to only a small number.[5]

1. Discuss Simon's story of praying several times to accept Jesus but not experiencing a transformed life (pages 4–7).

Read Matthew 7:13–14 and Matthew 7:21–23.

2. What did you learn about the "many" and the "few" in these verses?

3. What was the proof that Simon was truly born again? (See the bottom of page 6 in the book.)

> The rich young ruler came to Jesus with urgency—he came running.
> He came with humility—he came kneeling.
> Jesus loved him—yet he didn't chase after him.[6]

4. The rich young ruler was seeking eternal life. Why do you think Jesus made it so hard for him?

5. Why do you think Jesus didn't chase after the rich young ruler?

6. What do you think is the danger of pressuring someone to make an immediate decision for Christ?

7. What was Jesus' motivation for spending time with sinners? (See Luke 5:32, 1 Tim. 1:15.)

8. What has God taught you through this week's study?

"

In light of the sober possibility of profession without possession, the New Testament exhorts us to examine ourselves, to see if we are in the faith, to make our calling and election sure (2 Cor. 13:5). We have a moral obligation to encourage others to do likewise.

—William Webster[7]

STUDY NOTES

WEEK TWO

---

disciple
(noun)

Student: when fully trained
will be like his/her teacher.[1]

DAY 1

Read Chapter 3, "Follow Me" (pages 25–31).

> Our love for Christ must be so extremely great that any
> other affections would appear as hatred by comparison.

1. Do you feel that the statement above is too extreme? Explain your answer.

*2. What or whom does your life show you love the most? Yourself? Another person? A cause? Possessions? Or Jesus?

3. What is the proof that we are true disciples? (See John 15:8.)

DAY 2

1. In the Gospels, Jesus makes some very bold statements about who can and who cannot be his disciples. To be a disciple of Jesus, what must you do?

Luke 14:26 _____

Luke 14:27 _____

Luke 14:33 _____

*2. What would it look like in your life for you to do what Jesus calls us to do as his disciples?

3. What do you think it means to "count the cost" before you become a disciple of Jesus?

Jesus told the rich young ruler to sell all that he had and give to the poor before following. The man went away sorrowful. Jesus explained to his disciples how difficult it is for a rich person to enter the kingdom of God. The disciples were astonished by this and asked, "Then who can be saved?" (Mark 10:26).

Perhaps that's how you're feeling after considering what Jesus is asking you to give up. Take heart, Jesus' answer to his disciples is his answer for us as well.

4. Write out Mark 10:27.

5. Many of Jesus' early followers found his sayings hard to take and left him. Not so Peter. What made the cost of following Jesus worth it for him? (See John 6:68.)

Peter—A Case Study

1. What do we learn about Peter from Matthew 4:18–20?

2. What character quality does Peter show a lot of in Matthew 14:25–29?

3. As this account progresses in Matthew 14:30–32, what character quality does Peter reveal to have little of?

The night before Jesus died, Peter declared, "Though they all fall away because of you, I will never fall away" (Matt. 26:33). And "Even if I must die with you, I will not deny you" (Matt. 26:35). Not long after this bold declaration, Peter denied Jesus three times (Matt. 26:69–74).

4. What did Peter do once he recognized his sin (Matt. 26:75)?

After Jesus rose from the dead, he appeared to some of the disciples on the shore of the sea of Tiberius. As soon as Peter realized that it was the Lord, he jumped into the water to make his way quickly to Jesus. After they had eaten, Jesus turned to Peter and asked him, "Do you love me more than these?" (John 21:15). Three times, Jesus asked Peter, "Do you love me?" Just as Peter had denied Jesus three times, Jesus gave Peter the opportunity to publicly affirm his love three times.

5. Jesus also gave Peter the charge to "Feed my lambs," "Tend my sheep," and "Feed my sheep." Why do you think Jesus did that? (See John 21:15–17.)

We learn from Peter's life that the path of discipleship is not without failure. Peter was genuinely willing to go to prison or even die for His Lord (Luke 22:33), but not able to follow through because of human frailty. Then in the book of Acts we meet a changed Peter, a Peter who would one day, as history records, be martyred for his faith.

6. To what can we attribute the change?

Acts 1:8 _____

_____

Acts 4:13 _____

_____

7. Do you relate to Peter? If so, in what ways? If not, why not?

What changed Peter is the key to our change also. You may be willing to bear the cost of following Jesus but have doubts as to whether you are able. None of us is able. What made the difference for Peter is what will make the difference for you and me—the power of God in the person of the Holy Spirit.

DAY 4

Read chapter 4, "Examine Your Belief" (pages 33–37).

1. What claim does Jesus make in John 14:6? Do you believe this to be true?

2. What must I believe about myself to be saved? (See Romans 3:23; 1 John 1:8.)

3. What must I believe about who Jesus is to be saved? (See John 20:31; Romans 10:9, John 8:24; 10:30–33.)

For by grace you have been saved through faith. And this is not your own doing; it is the gift of God, not a result of works, so that no one may boast. For we are his workmanship, created in Christ Jesus for good works, which God prepared beforehand that we should walk in them.

—Ephesians 2:8–10

1. What are we saved by, according to Ephesians 2:8?

2. What are we not saved by according to Ephesians 2:9?

3. What are we saved for, according to Ephesians 2:10?

4. What does the Bible say will be the evidence of saving faith? (See James 2:17–18, 26; Matthew 3:8.)

5. To be a Christian, do we have to believe in the resurrection of Jesus from the dead? (See Rom. 4:25; Rom. 10:9.)

*SELF-EXAMINATION

Reflect on what you have read, studied, and learned in this week's lesson and record what your self-examination has revealed to you about your salvation. Record your answers and explain why.

Assurance :

Doubt :

Concern :

66

It is not my aim to introduce doubts and fears into your mind; no, but I do hope self-examination may help to drive them away. It is not security, but false security, which we would kill; not confidence, but false confidence, which we would overthrow; not peace, but false peace, which we would destroy.

—Charles Spurgeon[2]

1. Does the story of Jack sound unlikely? How do you think a situation like his could happen? (See page 33 in the book.)

Read Matthew 4:19; Luke 5:27–28 and Luke 9:23.

When Jesus called someone to be his disciple he used the words, "follow me." The above verses are just a few of the many instances when Jesus called people to follow him.

2. What is the significance of the words "follow me"?

3. What is the significance of the word "everything" (Luke 5:28)?

We can't pick and choose the teachings that suit us. Some commands will require sacrifice or be uncomfortable. A disciple must defer to the teacher and submit to his will in everything.

4. The Hebrew word for disciple is *talmid* (student). What are the qualities found in a good student?

> To the Hebrew mind, "making disciples" was a seamless reality, a continuous process that started with conversion and progressed teaching followers of Jesus Christ to obey all that he commanded.[3]
>
> —Doug Greenwold

Read Romans 10:9–10

5. What do these verses say is the result of believing?

6. According to the following verses, who believes that Jesus is the Son of God (Mark 3:11; Luke 4:41)?

7. Does that belief save them? (See Matt. 25:41.)

8. Both Judaism and Islam believe there is one God. Can that belief save them? Why or why not?

9. What has God taught you through this week's study?

"

Repentance is the hand releasing those filthy objects it had previously clung to so tenaciously. Faith is extending an empty hand to God to receive His gift of grace. Repentance is a godly sorrow for sin. Faith is receiving a sinner's Saviour. Repentance is revulsion of the filth and pollution of sin. Faith is a seeking of cleansing therefrom. Repentance is the sinner covering his mouth and crying, "Unclean, unclean!" Faith is the leper coming to Christ and saying, "Lord, if You will, You can make me clean."

—Arthur Pink[4]

STUDY NOTES

WEEK THREE

---

repentance
(noun)

A change of mind and heart
leading to a change of behavior.[1]

DAY 1

Read chapter 5, "Repentance—the Missing Note" (pages 39–44).

1. Define repentance (page 42).

*2. Does your life show the fruit of repentance? If so, what have you repented of?

3. Why do you think repentance is not a popular message?

The thread of repentance is woven throughout the New Testament. Look at the following verses that are a sampling of the many incidences where repentance was called for.

1. Who is calling for repentance in each passage?

Matthew 3:2 _____

Matthew 4:17 _____

Mark 6:7, 12 _____

Acts 17:30 _____

2. Who is being called to repent in Acts 17:30?

3. Although the literal definition of repent is "a change of mind," how does Matthew 3:8 help clarify what is the result?

Judas—A case study

For three years the twelve disciples walked with Jesus. They shared meals together with Jesus, listened to him preach, and witnessed him performing miracles.

Eventually, they too were sent out to preach and perform miracles.

> And he called the twelve and began to send them out two by two, and gave them authority over the unclean spirits . . . So they went out and proclaimed that people should repent. And they cast out many demons and anointed with oil many who were sick and healed them.
>
> —Mark 6:7, 12–13

1. Judas was one of the twelve disciples chosen by Jesus. According to the above verses, what activities was Judas involved in during the ministry of Jesus?

At the last supper Jesus predicted his betrayal (John 13:20).

> After saying these things, Jesus was troubled in his spirit, and testified, "Truly, truly, I say to you, one of you will betray me." The disciples looked at one another, uncertain of whom he spoke. One of his disciples, whom Jesus loved, was reclining at table at Jesus' side, so Simon Peter motioned to him to ask Jesus of whom he was speaking. So that disciple, leaning back against Jesus, said to him, "Lord, who is it?" Jesus answered, "It is he to whom I will give this morsel of bread when I have dipped it." So when he had dipped the morsel, he gave it to Judas, the son of Simon Iscariot. Then after he had taken the morsel, Satan entered into him. Jesus said to him, "What you are going to do, do quickly." Now no one at the table knew why he said this to him. Some thought that, because Judas had the moneybag, Jesus was telling him, "Buy what we need for the feast," or that he should give something to the poor.
>
> —John 13:21–29

Answer the following questions using John 13:21–29.

2. Did the other disciples suspect that Judas would betray Jesus?

3. What job did Judas have among the disciples? (See John 12:6.)

Judas was a trusted and active disciple of Jesus. Even those closest to him were deceived into believing he was something that he was not—a true disciple.

> When Judas, who had betrayed him, saw that Jesus was condemned, he was seized with remorse and returned the thirty pieces of silver to the chief priests and the elders. "I have sinned," he said, "for I have betrayed innocent blood."
>
> —Matthew 27:3–5 (NIV)

4. How did Judas respond to his sin of betrayal? (See above verses.)

> Godly sorrow brings repentance that leads to salvation and leaves no regret, but worldly sorrow brings death.
>
> —2 Corinthians 7:10 (NIV)

5. How do we know that Judas experienced worldly sorrow, not godly sorrow? (See John 17:12.)

DAY 4

Read chapter 6, "Strange Fruit" (pages 47–53).

1. Make a list of the bad fruit in Galatians 5:19–21.

2. If you notice that you often fall into one or more of these sins, what should you do?

3. What does the passage say will happen to people who live like this?

4. List the fruit of the Spirit in Galatians 5:22–25. Which fruit of the Spirit are evidenced in your life?

Read the parable found in Matthew 13:1–23.

*1. How would you characterize the soil of your heart? Is it hardened, rocky, full of weeds, or fertile ground? Explain your answer.

*2. Jesus said that the "cares of this world" choke the word in our hearts. What cares or anxieties weigh you down?

3. Jesus also said that the deceitfulness of riches chokes out the word in our hearts. In what ways are riches deceitful?

4. How do you think we can make the soil of our hearts more receptive to God's Word? (Some Scriptures to consider: Prov. 28: 13–14; Heb. 4:7; 2 Tim. 3:16–17; James 1:19.)

*SELF-EXAMINATION

Reflect on what you have read, studied, and learned in this week's lesson and record what your self-examination has revealed to you about your salvation. Record your answers and explain why.

Assurance :

Doubt :

Concern :

O what efforts Satan puts forth to keep people from this vitally important and all-necessary work of self-examination. He knows full well that if many of his deceived victims set about the task in earnest, they would soon discover that no miracle of Divine grace has been wrought in them, and that this would cause them to seek the Lord with all their hearts.

—A. W. Pink[2]

1. Read and discuss the analogy given by Ray Comfort in his *Way of the Master* evangelism training videos (pages 39–40).

Read Luke 24:45–47.

2. What encouragement do you receive from verse 45?

3. What in verse 46 is foundational to Christianity (cf. 1 Cor. 15:17)?

4. According to verse 47, what is an essential part of the gospel message?

5. List the characteristics of godly sorrow found in 2 Corinthians 7:9–11.

6. Can a true believer live a life with no fruit of the Spirit in evidence? Why or why not?

7. What must a person do to ensure a fruitful life? (See John 15:4–6.)

8. Share the most significant truth you gained in your study this week.

"

Saving faith is always fruitful; and that faith which is not fruitful is not true faith. The apostle does not deny that we are justified by faith, and only by faith; but he denies that faith without works is a true faith. It is only an empty notion; and such a faith cannot justify nor save a man.

—Thomas Senior[3]

STUDY NOTES

WEEK FOUR

---

confess
(verb)

To say the same thing as another.[1]
When I confess my sin, I agree with
God that what he calls sin really is sin.[2]

DAY 1

Read chapter 7, "Confession" (pages 55–62).

1. Define confession (page 56).

Translated from the Greek: _____

_____

In other words: _____

_____

*2. What things in your life that God calls sin are you making excuses for?

3. What's the difference between confession and repentance?

DAY 2

*1. What is your response when confronted with sin?

*2. Are you willing to confess and repent of your sin? What would repentance look like in your life?

3. Why is sin a heart issue, not merely an outward issue? (See Matt. 15:18–19; Luke 6:45.)

*4. In the book, I write, "A confession with an explanation is no confession at all."[5] Describe situations in your life when you are tempted to make excuses.

> If we claim to be without sin, we deceive ourselves and the truth is not in us. If we confess our sins, he is faithful and just and will forgive us our sins and purify us from all unrighteousness. If we claim we have not sinned, we make him out to be a liar and his word is not in us.
>
> —1 John 1:8–10

Review the definition of confession (Day 1), then read 1 John 1:8 and Luke 5:32.

1. Before we confess our sin what must we do first?

2. What happens when we confess our sins? (See 1 John 1:9.)

3. What does God's faithfulness have to do with my forgiveness? (See Rom. 10:9; Heb. 6:18; Heb. 13:8.)

4. What does God's justice have to do with my forgiveness? (Rom. 6:23; 5:8–10; 1 Peter 3:18.)

DAY 4

Read Chapter 8, "Forgiveness" (pages 65–72).

*1. Is there something in your life that you feel God can't forgive you for?

2. According to 1 John 1:9, how much unrighteousness is God willing to forgive?

*3. Think of something that God has forgiven you for and thank him.

1. Why do you think God *commands* us to forgive, rather than making it optional? (See Eph. 4:32; Col. 3:13; Matt. 6:14.)

2. Does forgiveness condone or excuse an offense? Why or why not?

*3. Being forgiven ourselves frees us to forgive others. Is there someone you need to forgive? Write a prayer asking God to help you forgive.

*SELF-EXAMINATION

Reflect on what you have read, studied, and learned in this week's lesson and record what your self-examination has revealed to you about your salvation. Record your answers and explain why.

Assurance :

Doubt :

Concern :

" "

Examine yourselves. You have seen the witness in the box, when the lawyer has been examining him, or, as we have it, cross-examining him. Now, mark: never was there a rogue less trustworthy or more deceitful than your own heart, and as when you are cross-examining a dishonest person— one that hath bye-ends to serve, you set traps for him to try and find him out in a lie, so do with your own heart. Question it backward and forward, this way and that way; for if there be a loophole for escape, if there be any pretence for self-deception, rest assured your treacherous heart will be ready enough to avail itself of it.

—Charles Spurgeon[4]

1. What is the difference between the confessions of Lance Armstrong and Felicity Huffman (pages 59-60 in the book)?

Read Psalms 51:2–4, 17 (See the bottom of page 56 in the book.)

2. What does David admit to in this Psalm?

3. What does David conclude is the proper response to his sin?

4. David was an adulterer and murderer, yet he was called a man after God's own heart. Regardless of what you have done, how do you think you can be a man/woman after God's own heart?

5. What was it that gave Corrie ten Boom the courage to forgive the prison guard? (See the top of page 68.)

Read Matthew 18:21–22

6. How many times are we to forgive someone who sins against us?

7. How do these verses relate to the topic of forgiveness?

8. What has God taught you through this week's study?

God never showed his hatred of sin so much as he did in Christ. When God sent his Son into the world to die for man's sin, he is saying, "they shall see the extent to which I hate sin in how I deal with my son."

—Jeremiah Burroughs[5]

STUDY NOTES

WEEK FIVE

obey
(verb)

To do what you are told or expected
to do according to someone in
authority or a rule or law.[1]

Read chapter 9, "Examine Your Obedience" (pages 75–82).

DAY 1

1. How can you know that you know God? (See 1 John 2:3.)

*2. Do you have this assurance?

*3. Are there areas in your life in which you know you're being disobedient to God?

4. What should be the motivation for our obedience to Christ (John 14:15; 1 John 5:3)?

DAY 2

1. Why is doing more important than just saying?

2. If our faith leaves us unchanged what does that say about our faith?

3. How did Noah and Abraham manifest their faith? (See Heb. 11:7–8.)

And to whom was God speaking when he took an oath that they would never enter his rest? Wasn't it the people who disobeyed him? So we see that because of their unbelief, they were not able to enter his rest.

—Hebrews 3:18–19 NLT

4. What kept the Israelites from entering God's rest? (See above verses.)

DAY 3

Read chapter 10, "Examine Your Loves" (pages 85–95).

*1. What would you say are your top three loves?

*2. If someone were to observe your life would their evaluation of your top three loves be consistent with yours?

3. What does Scripture tell us about loving the world? (1 John 2:15)

1. Using the following verses as a guide, make a list of questions to ask yourself before viewing entertainment or listening to music (1 Corinthians 10:23, 31; Philippians 4:8; Matthew 5:28).

*2. Have you ever compromised your beliefs or disobeyed God to save money? If so, bring it to God and ask his forgiveness.

*3. Is there an area of your life in which you have a hard time doing the right thing when no one's looking?

1. What does it mean to be conformed to the pattern of this world? (See Rom. 12:2.)

*2. List some ways that your choices are informed by Scripture.

*3. List ways that your choices are influenced by the world.

4. What do you think it means to "be transformed by the renewing of your mind?"

5. What is the goal of this transformation? (See 2 Cor. 3:18.)

*SELF-EXAMINATION

Reflect on what you have read, studied, and learned in this week's lesson and record what your self-examination has revealed to you about your salvation. Record your answers and explain why.

Assurance :

Doubt :

Concern :

"

The gospel Jesus proclaimed was a call to discipleship, a call to follow Him in submissive obedience, not just a plea to make a decision or pray a prayer. Jesus' message liberated people from the bondage of their sin while it confronted and condemned hypocrisy. It was an offer of eternal life and forgiveness for repentant sinners, but at the same time it was a rebuke to outwardly religious people whose lives were devoid of true righteousness. It put sinners on notice that they must turn from sin and embrace God's righteousness. It was in every sense good news, yet it was anything but easy-believism.

—John MacArthur[2]

GROUP STUDY QUESTIONS

1. What impact did reading God's Word have in Natalie's life? (See pages 76-80.)

> And we can be sure that we know him if we obey his commandments.
>
> —1 John 2:3

Read 1 John 2:3.

2. According to this verse, obedience is something that I do. Does this verse teach a works-based salvation? Why or why not?

3. What do we learn about obedience in 1 John 2:3?

> Whoever believes in the Son has eternal life; whoever does not obey the Son shall not see life, but the wrath of God remains on him.
>
> —John 3:36

4. What do we learn about belief and obedience from John 3:36? (See above verse.)

5. What does it mean to "not love the world?"

6. Matthew 22:37–38 says, "You shall love the Lord your God with all your heart and with all your soul and with all your mind." How can we do this?

7. What stood out to you most in this week's study?

"

I commend solitude to any of you who are seeking salvation, first, that you may study well your case as in the sight of God. Few men truly know themselves as they really are. Most people have seen themselves in a looking-glass, but there is another looking-glass, which gives true reflections, into which few men look. To study one's self in the light of God's Word, and carefully to go over one's condition, examining both the inward and the outward sins, and using all the tests which are given us in the Scriptures, would be a very healthy exercise; but how very few care to go through it!

—C. H. Spurgeon[3]

STUDY NOTES

.

WEEK SIX

---

die

(verb)

To stop living;
pass from physical life and lose all
bodily attributes and functions
necessary to sustain life.[1]

DAY 1

Read Chapter 11, "Dying to Self" (pages 97–103).

1. What must happen before a seed can bear fruit (John 12:24)?

2. What does it mean to die to self?

3. What does that look like for you?

DAY 2

I have been crucified with Christ. It is no longer I who live, but Christ who lives in me. And the life I now live in the flesh I live by faith in the Son of God, who loved me and gave himself for me.

—Galatians 2:20

1. Who and what is crucified with Christ? (See Gal. 5:24; 6:14.)

*2. Has there been a cost for you to follow Christ? If you are just now counting the cost, what will it be?

*3. Is there an area of your life where it has been hard to die to self? Describe this.

4. Why must our relationship with Christ come first in our lives?

DAY 3

Read Chapter 12, "Those Who Counted the Cost" (pages 105–113).

*1. Would you still be willing to follow Jesus if that decision resulted in any of the following:

	YES	NO
■ Suffering or trials	▨	▨
■ Being mistreated by others	▨	▨
■ Having your reputation damaged	▨	▨
■ Changing your social life	▨	▨
■ Changing how you spend your money	▨	▨
■ Losing your friends	▨	▨
■ Losing your job	▨	▨
■ Being disowned by your family	▨	▨
■ Losing your life	▨	▨

*2. How much are you willing to sacrifice to follow Jesus?

DAY 4

Read Philippians 1:29.

1. What is implied by the word "granted?"

2. What is granted in this verse?

3. How is it a privilege to suffer for Christ?

4. Read the following verses and record what a disciple of Jesus can expect: 2 Timothy 3:12; John 15:18.

DAY 5

1. What are some of the costs of being a disciple of Jesus?

Luke 14:26 _____

_____

_____

_____

Luke 14:27 _____

_____

_____

_____

Luke 14:33 _____

_____

_____

_____

Phil. 1:29 _____

_____

_____

_____

2. What are some of the benefits of being a disciple of Jesus?

John 1:12 _____

_____

_____

_____

Gal. 2:20 _____

_____

_____

_____

Phil. 3:7–8 _____

_____

_____

_____

Rom. 8:17 _____

_____

_____

_____

*SELF-EXAMINATION

Reflect on what you have read, studied, and learned in this week's lesson and record what your self-examination has revealed to you about your salvation. Record your answers and explain why.

Assurance :

Doubt :

Concern :

"

The cross is laid on every Christian. The first Christ-suffering which every man must experience is the call to abandon the attachments of this world. It is that dying of the old man which is the result of his encounter with Christ. As we embark upon discipleship we surrender ourselves to Christ in union with his death—we give over our lives to death. Thus it begins; the cross is not the terrible end to an otherwise God-fearing and happy life, but it meets us at the beginning of our communion with Christ. When Christ calls a man, he bids him come and die.

—Dietrich Bonhoeffer[2]

GROUP STUDY QUESTIONS

1. What cost did Rosaria Butterfield pay to follow Jesus (pages 108–111)?

Read Luke 9:57–62

2. Two of the three people in this account said, "I will follow you, Lord, but let me first..." How might someone today finish that sentence?

3. As with the rich young ruler, Jesus makes it difficult for his would-be disciples. What can we learn from this?

4. Read 2 Corinthians 11:23–29 and list some ways that Paul suffered for Christ.

5. Read 2 Corinthians 4:17–18. How does Paul view his troubles?

6. What cost was Jesus willing to pay for your salvation?

Mark 15:3–4 _____

_____

John 19:1–3 _____

_____

Philippians 2:6–8 _____

_____

1 Peter 2:24 _____

_____

Isaiah 52:14 _____

_____

Isaiah 53:3, 5–8 _____

_____

Psalms 41:9 _____

_____

"

Christianity consists not merely in speculation, but in practice. We must not only give our assent to the truth of the gospel, but give up our hearts to Christ. The faith which he requires is not a slight superficial belief that he is the Redeemer of mankind, but such a faith as will form us into subjection and obedience to himself.

—Jonathan Dickinson[4]

STUDY NOTES

WEEK SEVEN

---

greed

(noun)

Intense and selfish desire for
something, especially wealth,
power, or food.[1]

Read chapter 13, "The Gospel of Greed" (pages 115–122).

DAY 1

1. According to Colossians 3:5 and Ephesians 5:5, what is another word for greed?

2. What is the opposite of greed? (See 1 Tim. 6:18.)

*3. In what ways has the love of money affected your relationships with others? Consider the answer to this question in light of your answers for questions 1 and 2.

DAYS 2 AND 3

Read chapter 14, "The Gospel of Self" (pages 125–136).

1. What's the problem with sermons that are predominately motivational speeches?

2. Do you think Jesus would feel comfortable in the type of churches mentioned in this chapter? Why or why not?

3. Where is your treasure? (See Matt. 6:19–21.)

*4. How do you respond when you don't get what you think you deserve?

5. What's the danger of a me-centered gospel?

DAYS 4 AND 5

Read Chapter 15, "The Gospel of Rome" (pages 139–152).

According to *The Question and Answer Catholic Catechism,* "Both Sacred Scripture and Sacred Tradition are the inspired word of God, and both are forms of divine revelation."[1]

1. How would you respond to the above statement biblically? (Some Scriptures to consider: 2 Peter 1:20-21; 2 Timothy 3:16-17; Mark 7:8–9; Matt. 15:9; Acts 17:11.)

The *Catholic Encyclopedia* states

"Penance is a sacrament of the New Law instituted by Christ in which forgiveness of sins committed after baptism is granted through the priest's absolution to those who with true sorrow confess their sins and promise to satisfy for the same."[2]

2. Based on the above, what is penance supposed to accomplish?

3. Based on the quote from the Catholic Encyclopedia, through whom is this accomplished?

4. To whom is forgiveness of sins granted according to this Catholic teaching on penance?

5. According to the Bible, how is a person forgiven of their sins? (Some Scriptures to consider: Acts 10:43; Acts 3:19; 1 John 1:9; 1 Tim 2:5.)

The catechism of the Catholic Church, states: "The Church affirms that for believers, the sacraments of the New Covenant are necessary for salvation."[5]

6. Are there any examples from the Bible of people being saved without the sacraments?

7. What has God taught you through this week's study?

*SELF-EXAMINATION

Reflect on what you have read, studied, and learned in this week's lesson and record what your self-examination has revealed to you about your salvation. Record your answers and explain why.

Assurance :

Doubt :

Concern :

"

We should never be afraid to examine ourselves. But when doubts do arise, the solution is not to try harder to prove to ourselves that we are believers. The solution is to flee to the cross and to the righteousness of Christ, which is our only hope. And then, having looked to Christ alone for our justification, we can look to His Spirit to enable us to deal with those areas of our lives that cause doubt.

—Jerry Bridges[2]

1. Do you think there is a problem with preachers, such as Joel Osteen, whose messages focus on what God can do for us (pages 125–136)?

Read 2 Peter 2:3; Galatians 1:9

2. How does God respond to false teaching and false teachers?

3. What are some things that people add to the gospel?

4. How does adding to the gospel take away from the gospel?

5. What are some things that people take away from the gospel?

Read 2 Timothy 4:3–4.

6. What will some people not endure? What will they do instead?

7. What will they turn away from? What will they turn to?

8. What stood out to you the most in this week's study?

If the Bible teaches you something contrary to your theological view, you change your view and follow the Scripture, which will never contradict itself.

—C. Matthew McMahon[3]

STUDY NOTES

WEEK EIGHT

---

darkness

(noun)

Darkness is the absence of light . . .
The moment that light leaves,
darkness returns.[1]

DAY 1

Read chapter 16, "Light versus Darkness" (pages 155–159).

1. What are the "deeds of darkness" listed in Ephesians 5:3–5, Galatians 5:19–21, 1 Corinthians 6:9–10, and Romans 13:12–14?

2. What is the warning given to those who persist in "deeds of darkness" (Gal. 5:21; 1 Cor. 6:9)?

DAY 2

1. How can we tell if we're walking in the light (1 John 1:5–7)?

*2. When you sin, do you sense the conviction of the Holy Spirit over what you've done?

3. What's the difference between committing a sin and having sin as the pattern of your life?

4. According to John 3:19, why do people love darkness rather than light?

5. What claim and what promise does Jesus make in John 8:12?

Read chapter 17, "The Mystery of Salvation" (pages 161–168).

1. What good works did Mr. Haslam count on to ensure his right standing with God before he was converted (page 163 in the book)?

2. How do we know that these good works, and others, are not enough to earn favor with God?

Isaiah 64:6 _____

_____

_____

Ephesians 2:8–9 _____

_____

_____

Titus 3:4–5 _____

_____

_____

DAY 4

Read chapter 18, "The Wrath of God" (pages 171–179).

1. Define wrath.

2. According to 1 Thessalonians 5:9, for what is a believer *not* destined?

3. For what is a believer destined?

DAY 5

1. What are some sins God hates, and that cause his wrath? (See pages 173–175 in the book.)

2 Kings 22:13; Ephesians 5:5–6 _____

_____

Jeremiah 44:8; Colossians 3:5–6 _____

_____

Joshua 22:20 _____

_____

2 Chronicles12:12 _____

_____

Jeremiah 10:25 _____

_____

Romans 1:18 _____

_____

*2. Is your life characterized by behaviors that will incur the wrath of God?

*SELF-EXAMINATION

Reflect on what you have read, studied, and learned in this week's lesson and record what your self-examination has revealed to you about your salvation. Record your answers and explain why.

Assurance :

Doubt :

Concern :

"

Examine yourselves. Go right through yourselves from the beginning to the end. Stand not only on the mountains of your public character, but go into the deep valleys of your private life. Be not content to sail on the broad river of your outward actions, but go follow back the narrow rill till you discover your secret motive. Look not only at your performance, which is but the product of the soil, but dig into your heart and examine the vital principle. "Examine yourselves." This is a very big word—a word that needs thinking over; and I am afraid there be very few, if any of us, who ever come up to the full weight of this solemn exhortation— "Examine yourselves."

—Charles Spurgeon[2]

GROUP STUDY QUESTIONS

1. What was the evidence of conversion in Mr. Hardie's life (pages 165–167)?

2. What does it mean to walk in darkness? (Refer to your answers on Day 1, question 1.)

Read Romans 5:8–10

3. What does this passage teach us about God's wrath?

4. How do wrath and love meet in God's character?

5. What does the Bible teach us about God's anger?

Psalm 103:8 _____

_____

Deuteronomy 9:7 _____

_____

Romans 1:18 _____

_____

Romans 2:5 _____

_____

John 3:36 _____

_____

6. How can we be sure of avoiding God's wrath at the end of time? (See 1 Thess. 1:9–10, 1 Thess. 5:9; Rom. 5:9.)

7. What has God taught you through this week's study?

You cannot meet the risen Christ and just go on your merry way.

You cannot meet the risen Christ and your life be the same.

You cannot meet the risen Christ and you not be dramatically transformed.

If not, you have not met the risen Christ.

—Steven J. Lawson[3]

STUDY NOTES

WEEK NINE

reveal

(verb)

To allow something to be seen that,
until then, had been hidden.[1]

DAY 1

Read chapter 19, "The Great Reveal" (pages 181–189).

1. Can a person walk away from a genuine faith in Jesus? Explain your answer (1 John 2:19).

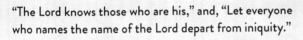

> "The Lord knows those who are his," and, "Let everyone who names the name of the Lord depart from iniquity."
>
> —2 Timothy 2:19

2. What will keep us out of heaven? (See Matt. 7:23; 2 Tim. 2:19; John 3:18; Luke 13:3.)

Read chapter 20, "The Gospel Changes Everything"
(pages 191–203).

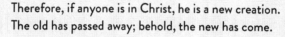

> Therefore, if anyone is in Christ, he is a new creation. The old has passed away; behold, the new has come.
>
> —2 Corinthians 5:17

1. The word "therefore" in the above verse refers to 2 Corinthians 5:14–16. According to those verses, what must happen before a person can become a new creation (cf. Gal. 2:20).

> Assuredly, I say to you, unless you are converted and become as little children, you will by no means enter the kingdom of heaven.
>
> —Matthew 18:3 (NKJV)

convert

(verb)

To change (something) into a
different form or properties;
transmute; transform.[2]

All true Christians are new creations and have been converted. The process of transformation will continue throughout our lives.

2. According to 2 Corinthians 3:18, what are we being converted (transformed) into?

*3. Are you more Christlike today than you were this time last year?

> "The mark of a believer is not the absence of sin,
> but the fact that we are fighting sin."[3]
>
> —John Piper

It's not about *perfection*—It's about *direction.*

DAY 4

Paul – A Case Study

Saul, as he was known when Jesus met him on the road to Damascus, was a Pharisee from Tarsus. He was a zealous follower of Judaism who sat under the teaching of Gamaliel, a famous Pharisee and rabbi (Acts 22:3).

1. Prior to his becoming a Christian, what do we know about Saul? (See Phil. 3:5–6; Acts 8:3.)

2. Acts 7 recounts the stoning of Stephen who was the first Christian martyr. What does Acts 7:58 tell us about Saul?

Saul received permission from the high priest to round up Christians in Damascus and bring them as prisoners to Jerusalem. While on his journey to Damascus, Saul had a dramatic encounter with Jesus.

> A light from heaven shone around him. And falling to the ground, he heard a voice saying to him, "Saul, Saul, why are you persecuting me?" And he said, "Who are you, Lord?" And he said, "I am Jesus, whom you are persecuting."
>
> —Acts 9:3–5

Saul was temporarily blinded in this encounter. After regaining his sight, he was baptized.

3. After spending some time with the disciples in Damascus, what is the first thing that Saul did? (See Acts 9:20.)

4. Paul was a man with a questionable past. How did he view himself (1 Tim. 1:15)?

5. Despite Paul's past, God used him mightily. Read 1 Timothy 1:16 and record any encouragement you receive from this verse.

DAY 5

Read chapter 21, "Nothing but the Truth" (pages 205–211).

1. Do you believe in absolute truth? Why or why not?

*2. When confronted with the truth, either in God's Word or from another person, are you more likely to let the truth change you, or do you spin the truth?

*3. Do you love the truth? If so, how does your life demonstrate that?

*4. What are you going to do about what you've read in this book?

*SELF-EXAMINATION

Reflect on what you have read, studied, and learned in this week's lesson and record what your self-examination has revealed to you about your salvation. Record your answers and explain why.

Assurance :

Doubt :

Concern :

The day of judgment will reveal strange things. The hopes of many, who were thought great Christians while they lived, will be utterly confounded. The rottenness of their religion will be exposed and put to shame before the whole world. It will then be proved, that to be saved means something more than "making a profession." We must make a "practice" of our Christianity as well as a "profession." Let us often think of that great day. Let us often "judge ourselves, that we be not judged," and condemned by the Lord.

—J. C. Ryle[4]

GROUP STUDY QUESTIONS

1. How do you think that someone like Charo Washer could be involved in so much Christian activity and not be saved (pages 182, 185–186)? Consider Matthew 7:21–23.

In Week 1 of this study, we looked at the Beatitudes, which are found at the very beginning of the Sermon on the Mount (Matt. 5–7). As our study ends, we will now look at the final words Jesus gave to the crowds gathered that day on the mountainside.

Read Matthew 7:24–27.

> Everyone then who hears these words of mine and does them will be like a wise man who built his house on the rock. And the rain fell, and the floods came, and the winds blew and beat on that house, but it did not fall, because it had been founded on the rock. And everyone who hears these words of mine and does not do them will be like a foolish man who built his house on the sand. And the rain fell, and the floods came, and the winds blew and beat against that house, and it fell, and great was the fall of it.
>
> —Matthew 7:24–27

2. What words is Jesus talking about and what does he want us to do with those words?

3. In what ways are the wise and foolish similar?

4. In what ways are the wise and foolish different?

> My sheep hear my voice, and I know them, and they follow me. I give them eternal life, and they will never perish, and no one will snatch them out of my hand.
>
> —John 10:27–28

5. Who are the sheep? What do we learn about them in John 10:27?

6. What does Jesus promise his sheep in John 10:28?

> Examine yourselves, to see whether you are in the faith. Test yourselves. Or do you not realize this about yourselves, that Jesus Christ is in you?—unless indeed you fail to meet the test!
>
> —2 Corinthians 13:5

Throughout this study we have been examining ourselves based on the truth of God's Word.

As mentioned in Week 1, self-examination can serve two purposes. It can bring assurance of salvation to the true believer, or it can cause doubt and healthy concern for the false convert.

If you passed the test, you can rest in the assurance of John 10:28: "I give them eternal life, and they will never perish, and no one will snatch them out of my hand."

If you failed the test, take heart, "today is the day of salvation." (2 Cor. 6:2) If God has revealed to you that you were trusting in a false hope, I urge you to not delay.

God wants us to have assurance that our sins are forgiven and that we have eternal life. John wrote his epistle for that very reason. "I write these things to you who believe in the name of the Son of God that you may know that you have eternal life" (1 John 5:13).

Many claim to know the Lord, but *few* are known by him. It is my prayer that each person reading this book will be among the few.

"

How happy will it be with you, if, after having searched yourself you can say, "I know in whom I have believed, and am persuaded that he is able to keep that which I have committed unto him." Why, then you will go along merrily and joyfully, because the search has had a good result. And what if it should have a bad result? Better that you should find it out now than find it out too late.

—Charles Spurgeon[5]

> "The man who has struggled to purify himself and has had nothing but repeated failures will experience real relief when he stops tinkering with his soul and looks away to the perfect One. While he looks at Christ, the very thing he has so long been trying to do will be getting done within him.

—A. W. Tozer[6]

STUDY NOTES

APPENDIX A

7 Tests of True Faith

Examine yourselves to see whether you are in the faith;
test yourselves . . . 2 Cor. 13:5

The Bible says, "Not everyone who says to me, 'Lord, Lord,' will enter the kingdom of heaven." That's why it's important that we, who claim to be Christians, examine ourselves.

A Christian is a follower of Christ. No one is born a Christian; to become one you must be born again (John 3:3). If you are truly born again there will be evidence (2 Cor. 5:17).

If you genuinely want to know where you stand with God, I urge you to take these tests.

1. BELIEF TEST

You cannot be saved without a correct belief, so to find assurance of your salvation it is important that *belief* be the first test.

The gospel is the good news that guilty sinners can be justified (made right with God) (Rom. 5:1).

BELIEVE: Biblical belief is more than an intellectual agreement with facts; it involves entrusting oneself to the object of belief, namely Jesus (John 1:12, John 3:16, John 3:36).

CONFESS: The literal definition is, "to say the same thing as another." In other words, when I confess my sin, I agree with God that what he calls sin really is sin (Rom. 10:9, 1 John 1:9).

REPENT: Literally "a change of mind." However, genuine repentance includes a change of heart leading to a change of behavior (Luke 5:32, Luke 24:47, Acts 3:19). Saving faith will include an acknowledgement of sin (confession), and a desire to turn from sin (repentance).

■ Do you believe the gospel message?

■ Have you acknowledged your sin and repented of it?

2. LOVE FOR GOD AND FOR OTHERS TEST

If you have a correct belief, then the proof of your salvation will be evident in who and what you love, and how you live.

Jesus said, "If you love me you will keep my commandments" (John 14:15; Luke 10:27).

Anyone who claims to be in the light but hates a brother or sister is still in the darkness (1 John 2:9, 1 John 4:16, 2 Tim. 3:1–5, John 3:14).

■ If someone were to list the things you love, where would God come on the list?

■ Do you love God's people and enjoy fellowship with them?

3. LOVE FOR THE WORLD TEST

"Do not love the world or anything in the world. If anyone loves the world, love for the Father is not in them. For everything in the world—the lust of the flesh, the lust of the eyes, and the pride of life—comes not from the Father but from the world" (1 John 2:15–16).

■ Where do your affections lie?

"If anyone is in Christ, he is a new creation. The old has passed away; behold, the new has come" (2 Cor. 5:17).

"If we claim to have fellowship with him and yet walk in the darkness, we lie and do not live out the truth. But if we walk in the light, as he is in the light, we have fellowship with one another, and the blood of Jesus, his Son, purifies us from all sin" (1 John 1:6–7).

The following verses describe the deeds of darkness: Rom. 13:12–14; 1 Cor. 6:9–11; Gal 5:19–21; Eph. 5:3–6.

- Are you walking in the light, or are you walking in darkness?
- Do you love the things that God hates?

5. OBEDIENCE TEST

"And we can be sure that we know him if we obey his commandments" (John 2:3; 1 John 2:4–6).

- Is your life characterized by obedience to God?
- Is there an area of your life that you are living in deliberate disobedience? If so, are you willing to repent and turn from your sin?

6. SIN TEST

"No one born of God makes a practice of sinning, for God's seed abides in him; and he cannot keep on sinning, because he has been born of God. By this it is evident who are the children of God, and who are the children of the devil: whoever does not practice righteousness is not of God, nor is the one who does not love his brother" (1 John 3:9–10).

- Are you living in habitual sin?
- Do you justify things in your life that God calls sin?

"You will recognize them by their fruits" (Matt. 7:20; Phil. 1:11; John 15:8).

"The fruit of the Spirit is love, joy, peace, patience, kindness, goodness, faithfulness, gentleness, self-control" (Gal. 5:22–23).

■ Fruit is the proof of a genuine disciple. Is the fruit of the spirit evident in your life?

> If your faith in Christ leaves you unchanged, you don't have saving faith. Obedience—not perfection, but a new direction of thought and affections and behavior—is the fruit that shows that the faith is alive. Faith alone justifies, but the faith that justifies is never alone. It is always accompanied by "newness of life" (Rom. 6:4) [1]
>
> —John Piper

Dear Reader, no one will be perfect on this side of heaven, but a genuine Christian will be striving to please God (Heb. 12:14; 1 Peter 1:15).

We are warned in Scripture to "not be deceived" (1 Cor. 6:9). Sadly, many who think they are saved will hear the words, "I never knew you, depart from me" (Matt. 7:23). Examine yourself to be sure that you will not be among that crowd.

It's not about trying harder to please God, it's about surrender and dying to self (Gal. 2:20–21). Salvation isn't earned, it is by grace through faith (Eph. 2:8–9; Rom. 11:6).

We are told that we can have assurance of salvation. After going through a series of tests, John ends his epistle with these words.

"I write these things to you who believe in the name of the Son of God that you may know that you have eternal life" (1 John 6:9). God wants us to have assurance.

"There is therefore now no condemnation for those who are in Christ Jesus" (Rom. 8:1).

" "

It is a preposterous assumption that for a man to know himself to be a sinner proves him to be a saint. Let me ask the physician whether a sense of sickness proves a man to be cured. Let me ask a drowning man whether a sense of sinking proves that he is rescued ... You know better; common sense teaches you better! It is not a discovery of your sin that will save you, but hearty faith in the Savior; and if you have not gone further than a mere conviction of sin, which may be nothing but a legal conviction, and a natural alarm at the awful punishment of sin—if you have not gone further than mere alarm or remorse, you have not the spot which marks you out to be a child of God ... A cutting truth is this, but it must be told, lest any are misled.

—C. H. Spurgeon[1]

APPENDIX B

SELF-EXAMINATION
A Sermon by Spurgeon

A SERMON DELIVERED ON, OCTOBER 10, 1858
BY C. H. SPURGEON AT THE MUSIC HALL,
ROYAL SURREY GARDENS

"Examine yourselves, whether ye be in the faith; prove your own selves. Know ye not your own selves, how that Jesus Christ is in you, except ye be reprobates." 2 Corinthians 13:5

I HAD intended to address you this morning from the third title given to our blessed Redeemer in the verse we have considered twice before, "Wonderful, Counsellor, the mighty God," but owing to excruciating pain and continual sickness, I have been unable to gather my thoughts together, and therefore, I feel constrained to address you on a subject which has often been upon my heart and not infrequently upon my lips, and concerning which, I dare say, I have admonished a very large proportion of this audience before.

You will find the text in the thirteenth chapter of the second epistle to the Corinthians, at the fifth verse, "Examine yourselves, whether ye be in the faith; prove your own selves. Know ye not your own selves, how that Jesus Christ is in you, except ye be reprobates?"*—a solemn text that we cannot preach too impressively or too frequently meditate upon.

The Corinthians were the critics of the apostles' age. They took to themselves great credit for skill in learning and in language, and as most men do who are wise in their own esteem, they made a wrong use of their wisdom and learning—they began to criticize the apostle Paul. They criticized his style. "His letters," say they, "are weighty and powerful, but his bodily presence is weak and his speech contemptible." Nay, not content with that, they went so far as to deny his apostleship, and for once in his life, the apostle Paul found himself compelled to "become a fool in glorying; for," says he, "ye have compelled me: for I ought to have been commended of you: for in nothing am I behind the very chiefest apostles, though I be nothing."

The apostle wrote two letters to them, in both he is compelled to upbraid them while he defends himself, and when he had fully disarmed his opponents and wrested the sword of their criticism out of their hands, he pointed it at their own breasts, saying, "'Examine yourselves.' You have disputed my doctrine, examine whether ye be in the faith. You have made me prove my apostleship, 'prove your own selves.' Use the powers which you have been so wrongfully exercising upon me for a little season upon your own characters."

And now, my dear friends, the fault of the Corinthians is the fault of the present age. Let not any one of you, as he goes out of the house of God, say unto his neighbor, "How did you like the preacher? What did you think of the sermon this morning?" Is that the question you should ask as you retire from God's house?

---

*The Greek word, *adokimos* is translated as *reprobate* in the KJV. Other versions translate the word to say, *fail the test, unapproved and disqualified.*

Do you come here to judge God's servants? I know it is but a small thing unto us to be judged of man's judgment, for our judgment is of the Lord our God—to our own Master we shall stand or fall. But O men! You should ask a question more profitable unto yourselves than this. You should say, "Did not such and such a speech strike me? Did not that exactly consort with my condition? Was that not a rebuke that I deserve, a word of reproof or of exhortation? Let me take unto myself that which I have heard, and let me not judge the preacher, for He is God's messenger to my soul. I came up here to be judged of God's Word, and not to judge God's Word myself." But since there is in all our hearts a great backwardness to self-examination, I shall lay out myself for a few minutes this morning, earnestly to exhort myself, and all of you, to examine ourselves whether we be in the faith. First, I shall expound my text. Secondly, I shall enforce it. And thirdly, I shall try and help you to carry it into practice here and on the spot.

I. First, I shall EXPOUND MY TEXT.

Though in truth it needs no exposition, for it is very simple, yet by studying it and pondering it, our hearts may become more deeply affected with its touching appeal. "Examine yourselves." Who does not understand that word? And yet, by a few suggestions you may know its meaning more perfectly.

"Examine"—that is a *scholastic idea*. A boy has been to school a certain time and his master puts him through his paces—questions him to see whether he has made any progress—whether he knows anything. Christian, catechize your heart. Question it to see whether it has been growing in grace. Question it to see if it knows anything of vital godliness or not. Examine it, pass your heart through a stern examination as to what it does know and what it does not know, by the teaching of the Holy Spirit.

Again it is a *military idea*. "Examine yourselves," or renew yourselves. Go through the rank and file of your actions and examine all your motives. Just as the captain on review day is not content with merely surveying the men from a distance, but must look at all their accoutrements, so do you look well to yourselves—examine yourselves with the most scrupulous care.

And once again, this is a *legal idea*. "Examine yourselves." You have seen the witness in the box, when the lawyer has been examining him, or as we have it, cross-examining him. Now, mark, never was there a rogue less trustworthy or more deceitful than your own heart, and as when you are cross examining a dishonest person—one that has bye-ends to serve, you set traps for him to try and find him out in a lie, so do with your own heart. Question it backward and forward, this way and that way, for if there be a loophole for escape, if there be any pretense for self-deception, rest assured your treacherous heart will be ready enough to avail itself of it.

And yet once more, this is a *traveler's idea*. I find in the original, it has this meaning, "Go right through yourselves." As a traveler, if he has to write a book upon a country, is not content to go round its borders merely, but goes, as it were, from Dan to Beersheba, right through the country. He climbs the hilltop, where he bathes his forehead in the sunshine. He goes down into the deep valleys, where he can only see the blue sky like a strip between the lofty summits of the mountains. He is not content to gaze upon the broad river unless he traces it to the spring whence it rises. He will not be satisfied with viewing the products of the surface of the earth, but he must discover the minerals that lie within its bowels.

Now, do the same with your heart. "Examine yourselves." Go right through yourselves from the beginning to the end. Stand not only on the mountains of your public character, but go into the deep valleys of your private life. Be not content to sail on the broad river of your outward actions, but go follow back the narrow rill till you discover your secret motive. Look not only at your performance, which is but the product of the soil, but dig into your heart and examine the vital principle. "Examine yourselves." This is a very big word—a word that needs thinking over. And I am afraid there are very few, if any of us, who ever come up to the full weight of this solemn exhortation, "Examine yourselves."

There is another word you will see a little further on, if you will kindly look at the text. "Prove your own selves." That means more than self-examination. Let me try to show the difference between the two. A man is about to buy a horse. He examines it. He looks at it. He thinks that possibly he may find out some flaw and therefore he carefully examines it. But after he has examined it, if he be a prudent man, he says to the person of whom he is about to buy, "I must prove this horse, will you let me have it for a week, for a month, or for some given time, that I may prove the animal before I actually invest in him?" You see, there is more in proof than in examination. It is a deeper word and goes to the very root and quick of the matter.

I saw but yesterday an illustration of this. A ship, before she is launched, is examined. When launched she is carefully looked at. And yet before she is allowed to go far out to sea, she takes a trial trip. She is proved and tried, and when she has roughed it a little, and it has been discovered that she will obey the helm, that the engines will work correctly, and that all is in right order, she goes out on her long voyages.

Now, "prove yourselves." Do not merely sit in your closet and look at yourselves alone, but go out into this busy world and see what kind of piety you have. Remember, many a man's religion will stand examination that will not stand proof. We may sit at home and look at our religion and say, "Well, I think this will do!" It is like cotton prints that you can buy in sundry shops. They are warranted fast colors and so they seem when you look at them, but they are not washable when you get them home. There is many a man's religion like that. It is good enough to look at and it has got the "warranted" stamped upon it, but when it comes out into actual daily life, the colors soon begin to run and the man discovers that the thing was not what he took it to be.

You know in Scripture we have an account of certain very foolish men that would not go to a great supper, but foolish as they were, there was one of them who said, "I have bought a yoke of oxen and I go to prove them." Thus he had at least worldly wisdom enough to test his oxen. So do you prove yourselves. Try to plow in the furrows of duty, see whether you can be accustomed to the yoke of Gospel servitude. Be not ashamed to put yourselves through your paces. Try yourself in the furnace of daily life, lest haply the mere examination of the chamber should detect you to be a cheat, and you should after all prove to be a castaway. "Examine yourselves; prove your own selves."

There is a sentence which I omitted, namely, this one, "Examine yourselves, whether ye be in the faith." "Oh!" says one, "you may examine me whether I am in the faith. I am an orthodox Christian, fully up to the standard, good genuine weight. There is no fear whatever of my coming up to the mark and going a little beyond it too." Ah! But my friend, that is not the question. I would have you orthodox, for a man who is heterodox in his opinions will most likely be heterodox in his actions. But the question now is not whether you believe the truth—but whether ye are in the truth?

Just to give you an illustration of what I mean. There is the ark and a number of men around it. "Ah!" says one, "I believe that ark will swim." "Oh!" says another, "I believe that ark is made of gopher wood and is strong from stem to stern. I am quite sure that ark will float, come what may. I am a firm believer in that ark." Ay, but when the rain descended and the flood came, it was not believing the ark as a matter of fact—it was being in the ark that saved men, and only those who were in it escaped in that dread day of deluge.

So there may be some of you that say of the Gospel of Christ, "I believe it to be of a particular character," and you may be quite correct in your judgment. You may say, "I think it to be that which honors God and casts down the pride of man." Herein too you may think quite right. But mark, it is not having an orthodox faith, but it is being in the faith, being in Christ, taking refuge in Him as in the ark. For he that only has the faith as a thing ab extra, [sic] and without being in the faith, shall perish in the day of God's anger. But he that lives by faith, he who feels that faith operates upon him, and is to him a living principle, he who realizes that faith is his dwelling place, that there he can abide, that it is the very atmosphere he breathes, and the very girdle of his loins to strengthen him—such a man is in the faith.

But we repeat again, all the orthodoxy in the world, apart from its effect upon the heart as a vital principle, will not save a man. "Examine yourselves, whether ye be in the faith; prove your own selves." "Know ye not your own selves?" If you do not, you have neglected your proper study. What avails all else that you do know, if you know not yourself? You have been roaming abroad, while the richest treasure was lying at home. You have been busying yourself with irrelevant affairs, while the main business has been neglected and ruined. "Know ye not your own selves?" And especially know you not this fact, that Jesus Christ must be in your heart, formed and living there, or else you are reprobates? That is, you are worthless persons, vain pretenders, spurious professors. Your religion is but a vanity and a show. "Reprobate silver shall men call you, because the Lord hath rejected you."

Now, what is it to have Jesus Christ in you? The Roman Catholic hangs the cross on his bosom. The true Christian carries the cross in his heart. And a cross inside the heart, my friends, is one of the sweetest cures for a cross on the back. If you have a cross in your heart—Christ crucified in you, the hope of glory—all the cross of this world's troubles will seem to you light enough and you will easily be able to sustain them. Christ in the heart means Christ believed in, Christ beloved, Christ trusted, Christ espoused, Christ communed with, Christ as our daily food, and ourselves as the temple and palace wherein Jesus Christ daily walks. Ah! there are many here that are total strangers to the meaning of this phrase. They do not know what it is to have Jesus Christ in them. Though you know a little about Christ on Calvary, you know nothing about Christ in the heart. Now, remember, that Christ on Calvary will save no man, unless Christ be in the heart. The Son of Mary, born in the manger, will not save a soul, unless He be also born in your hearts and live there—your joy, your strength, and your consolation. "Know ye not your own selves, how that Jesus Christ is in you, except ye be reprobates?"

II. The second point was to ENFORCE THE TEXT.

I have proved it. Now I am to enforce it. And here is the tug of war. May the Spirit of the living God drive the sword in up to its very hilt this morning, that now the power of God may be felt in every heart, searching and trying the reins. "Examine yourselves, whether ye be in the faith." "Examine yourselves," first, because it is a matter of the very highest importance. Small tradesmen may take coppers over the counter without much examination. But when it comes to gold, they will ring it well, for they could not afford to lose a sovereign out of their little gains. And if it comes to a five pound note, there is an anxious holding it up to the window to see if the watermark be there and whether all be correct, for it might be ruin to the man if he lost a sum to him so large.

Ah! But merchants and tradesmen, if you are deceived in the matter of your own souls, you are deceived indeed. Look well to the title deeds of your estate. Look well to your life insurance policies and to all the business that you do, but remember, all the gold and silver you have are but as the rack and scum of the furnace compared with the matter now in hand. It is your soul, your own soul, your never dying soul! Will you risk that? In times of panic, men will scarcely trust their fellows. I would to God there was a panic this day, so that no man would trust himself. You may trust your fellows far more safely than you may trust yourselves. Will you think, men and brethren, what your soul is? "The life is more than meat, and the body than raiment," but the soul is as much more to be accounted of than the body, as the body is more important than the raiment. Here are my clothes, let me be robbed of my garments. If my body is secure, what matters it? And as for my body, what is it, after all, but the rag that enshrines and covers my soul? Let that be sick, let that become like a worn-out vesture, I can afford to lose my body. But O God, I cannot afford to have my soul cast into hell. What a frightful hazard is that which you and I are running, if we do not examine ourselves! It is an everlasting hazard. It is a hazard of heaven or of hell, of God's eternal favor or of His everlasting curse. Well might the apostle say, "Examine yourselves."

Again, "Examine yourselves," because if you make a mistake you can never rectify it, except in this world. A bankrupt may have lost a fortune once and yet may make another. But make bankruptcy— spiritual bankruptcy in this life, and you will never have an opportunity to trade again for heaven. A great general may lose one battle, but with skill and courage he may retrieve his honor by winning another. But get defeated in the battle of this life and you can no more gird on your armor, you are defeated forever. The day is lost and there is no hope of your being able to gain it again or so much as to make the attempt. Now or never, man! Remember that. Your soul's eternal state hangs on the turn of today. Loiter your time away, waste your abilities, take your religion at second hand of your priest, of your minister, or of your friend, and in the next world you shall everlastingly rue the error, but you shall have no hope of amending it.

"Fix'd is their everlasting state,
Could man repent, 'tis then too late.
There are no acts of pardon pass'd
In the cold grave, to which we haste;
But darkness, death, and long despair,
Reign in eternal silence there."

"Examine yourselves," again, because many have been mistaken. That is a matter which I will undertake to affirm upon my own authority, certain that each one of you can confirm it by your own observation. How many in this world think themselves to be godly when they are not? You have in the circle of your own friends, persons making a profession, of whom you often stand in astonishment and wonder how they dare to do it. Friend, if others have been mistaken, may not you be? If some here and there fall into an error, may not you also do the same? Are you better than they? No, in nowise. You may be mistaken also. Methinks I see the rocks on which many souls have been lost—the rocks of presumption and the siren song of self-confidence entices you on to those rocks this morning. Stay, mariner, stay, I beseech you! Let yon bleached bones keep you back. Many have been lost, many are lost now, and are wailing at this present hour their everlasting ruin, and their loss is to be traced to nothing more than this, that they never examined themselves whether they were in the faith.

And here let me appeal to each person now present. Do not tell me that you are an old church member. I am glad to hear it, but still, I beseech you, examine yourself, for a man may be a professor of religion thirty or forty years, and yet there may come a trial-day when his religion shall snap after all and prove to be a rotten branch of the forest. Tell me not you are a deacon, that you may be, and yet you may be damnably deceived. Ay, and whisper not to me that you are a minister. My brethren in the ministry—we may lay aside our cassocks to wear belts of flames in hell. We may go from our pulpit, having preached to others what we never knew ourselves, and have to join the everlasting wailings of souls we have helped to delude. May God save us from such a doom as that! But let no man fold his arms and say, "I need not examine myself," for there is not a man here, or anywhere, who has not good cause to test and try himself today.

Furthermore, examine yourselves, because God will examine you. In the hand of God there is the scale and the balance. You shall not be taken into heaven for what you profess to be, but you shall be weighed—every one of you put into the scale. What a moment will that be with me and with you, when we are in God's great scale? Surely were it not for faith in the Lord Jesus Christ, and for a certainty that we shall be clothed in His righteousness at last, we might all tremble at the thought of ever being there, lest we should have to come out of the scale with this verdict, "Tekel"—("Mene, mene, tekel, upharsin")—"thou art weighed in the balances and art found wanting." God will not take His gold and silver by appearance, but every vessel must be purified in the fire. We must each one of us pass through a most searching test and scrutiny. Beloved, if our hearts condemn us, how much more shall God condemn us? If we are afraid to examine ourselves, what cause we have to tremble at the thought of the dread searching of God? Some of you feel that you are condemned this very day by a poor creature like myself, how much more, then, shall you be condemned when God, in thunder robed, shall summon you and all your fellows to the last infallible judgment? Oh! May God help us now to examine ourselves!

And I have yet one more reason to give. Examine yourselves, my dear friends, because if you are in doubt now, the speediest way to get rid of your doubts and fears is by self-examination. I believe that many persons are always doubting their eternal condition, because they do not examine themselves. Self-examination is the safest cure for one half the doubts and fears that vex God's people. Look at the captain over yonder. He is in his ship and he says to the sailors, "You must sail very warily and carefully, and be upon your watch, for to tell you the truth, I do not know where I am. I do not exactly know my latitude and longitude, and there may be rocks very close ahead and we may soon have the ship broken up." He goes down into the cabin, he searches the charts, he takes an inspection of the heavens, he comes up again, and he says, "Hoist every sail and go along as merrily as you please. I have discovered where we are. The water is deep and there is a wide sea room. There is no need for you to be in any trouble, searching has satisfied me." And how happy will it be with you, if after having searched yourself you can say, "I know in whom I have believed, and am persuaded that he is able to keep that which I have committed unto him." Why, then you will go along merrily and joyfully, because the search has had a good result. But what if it should have a bad result? Better that you should find it out now than find it out too late. One of the prayers I often pray and desire to pray as long as I live, is this, "Lord, let me know the worst of my case. If I have been living in a false comfort, Lord, rend it away. Let me know just what I am and where I am, and rather let me think too harshly of my condition before You than think too securely and so be ruined by presumption." May that be a prayer of each heart and be heard in heaven!

III.   And now, HOW ARE YOU TO SEARCH YOURSELVES?

I am to try and help you, though it must be very briefly. First, if you would examine yourselves, begin with your public life. Are you dishonest? Can you thieve? Are you given to drunkenness, uncleanness, blasphemy, taking God's name in vain? Make short work with yourself. There will be no need to go into any further tests. "He that doeth these things hath no inheritance in the kingdom of God." You are reprobate. The wrath of God abides on you. Your state is fearful. You are accursed now, and except you repent you must be accursed forever.

And yet, Christian, despite your many sins, can you say, "By the grace of God I am what I am, but I seek to live a righteous, godly, and sober life in the midst of a crooked and perverse generation." Remember, professor, by your works you shall be judged at last. Your works cannot save you, but they can prove that you are saved, or if they are evil works, they can prove that you are not saved at all. And here I must say, every one of us has good cause to tremble, for our outward acts are not what we would have them to be. Let us go to our houses and fall upon our face and cry again, "God be merciful to me a sinner!" And let us seek for more grace that henceforth our lives may be more consistent and more in accordance with the spirit of Christ.

Again another set of tests—private tests. How about your private life? Do you live without prayer, without searching the Scriptures? Do you live without thoughts of God? Can you live as a habitual stranger to the Most High, having no love to Him and no fear of Him? If so, I make short work of the matter—you are "in the gall of bitterness and in the bonds of iniquity." But if you are right at heart, you will be able to say, "I could not live without prayer. I have to weep over my prayers, but still I would weep ten times more if I did not pray. I do love God's Word, it is my meditation all the day. I love His people. I love His house and I can say that my hands are often lifted upward towards Him. And when my heart is busy with this world's affairs, it is often going up to His throne." A good sign, Christian, a good sign for you. If you can go through this test, you may hope that all is well. But go a little deeper. Have you ever wept over your lost condition? Have you ever bemoaned your lost estate before God? Say, have you ever tried to save yourself and found it a failure? And have you been driven to rely simply, wholly, and entirely on Christ? If so, then you have passed the test well enough. And have you now faith in Christ—a faith that makes you love Him, a faith that enables you to trust Him in the darkest hour? Can you say of a truth that you have a secret affection towards the Most High—that you love His Son, that your desire is after His ways, that you feel the influence of the divine Spirit, and seek every day to experience the fellowship of the Holy Spirit more and more?

And lastly, can you say that Jesus Christ is in you? If not, you are reprobate. Sharp though that word be, you are a reprobate. But if Jesus Christ be in your heart, though your heart sometimes be so dark that you can scarcely tell He is there, yet you are accepted in the Beloved and you may "rejoice with joy unspeakable and full of glory." I intended to have enlarged, but it is impossible for me to go further. I must therefore dismiss you with a sacred blessing. [1]

APPENDIX C

Assurance of Salvation

While a teenager I went through a period when I was deeply troubled with doubts regarding my salvation. I feared that I wasn't really saved, and this caused me great concern. To ease my doubts, I went through the New Testament and wrote down verses that had to do with salvation and made it like a checklist. I would read a verse, and ask myself, "Have I done what this verse says I must do to be saved?"

For example, after reading Acts 16:31, I would ask myself, "Do I believe in the Lord Jesus?" Luke 24:47 led me to ask if I had really repented for my sins.

Going through this process eventually gave me the peace that I was longing for.

While this book has dealt predominantly with evidence of salvation, our abiding hope and security doesn't ultimately come from what we do or don't do as a Christian. Our security rests in the promises of God.

> And this is the testimony, that God gave us eternal life, and this life is in his Son. Whoever has the son has life; whoever does not have the Son of God does not have life. I write these things to you who believe in the name of the Son of God, that you many know that you have eternal life.
>
> —1 John 5:11–13

Jesus himself gives assurance to those who believe in him: "I give them eternal life, and they shall never perish; no one can snatch them out of my hand" (John 10:28).

Salvation is by grace, through faith. "And this is not your own doing; it is the gift of God" (Eph. 2:8).

"While a change in lifestyle is evidence of saving faith, correct living without a changed heart makes you no better than the Pharisees".[1]

HERE ARE SOME QUESTIONS TO ASK YOURSELF:

Do you acknowledge that you are a sinner (Rom. 3:23)?

Do you believe that Jesus died, and rose again to pay the penalty for your sin (2 Cor. 5:21; 1 Cor. 15:3–4)?

Have you repented of your sin (Acts 3:19)?

Are you trusting in Christ alone for your salvation (Eph. 2:8–9)?

It is my prayer that through self-examination, you will be able to confidently say, "Yes! I am trusting in Christ alone for my salvation."

If you can't say that, there is no better time to trust Christ as Savior and Lord. Your eternal future depends on it."

NOTES

WEEK ONE

1 *Merriam-Webster,* s.v. "examine (v)," https://www.merriam-webster.com/dictionary/examine.

2 C.H. Spurgeon, "Self-Examination," (sermon 218, Music Hall, Royal Surrey Gardens, Newington, Surrey, London, October 10, 1858), https://www.spurgeongems.org/sermon/chs218.pdf.

3 A.W. Pink, *An Exposition of Hebrews,* "A Call to Examination," https://www.monergism.com/exposition-hebrews-ebook.

4 *Merriam-Webster,* s.v. "many, (adj.)," https://www.merriam-webster.com/dictionary/many

5 *Merriam-Webster,* s.v. "few, (adj)," https://www.merriam-webster.com/dictionary/few

6 Denise Wilson, *Seven Words You Never Want to Hear* (Enumclaw, WA: Redemption Press, 2021).

7 William Webster, "One, Holy, "Catholic," and Apostolic Church," *Tabletalk Magazine,* June 2004, 14. https://tabletalkmagazine.com/article/2004/06/one-holy-catholic-and-apostolic-church-3/

WEEK TWO

1 See Luke 6:40.

2 A.W. Pink, *Studies on Saving Faith,* https://www.monergism.com/studies-saving-faith-ebook.

3 Doug Greenwold, *Making Disciples Jesus' Way: Wisdom We Have Missed* (Gaithersburg, MD: Signature Book Printing, Inc., 2005), 21.

4 Arthur Pink, *A Fourfold Salvation,* https://www.chapellibrary.org/book/fsal

WEEK THREE

1   Wilson, *Seven Words,* 42.

2   "Devotionals: Morning and Evening: Evening Read", December 18, 2000, Blue Letter Bible, C. H. Spurgeon, https://www.blueletterbible.org/devotionals/me/view.cfm?Date=12%2F18&Time=pm&Date=.

3   Thomas Senior, et al. *A Biblical Guide to Hearing and Studying the Word of God,* (Crossville, TN: Puritan Publications, 2021) 77.

WEEK FOUR

1   *Strong's Greek Dictionary,* s.v. "homologeo," 3670.

2   Wilson, *Seven Words,* 56.

3   Wilson, *Seven Words,* 57.

4   C.H. Spurgeon, "Self-Examination," https://www.spurgeongems.org/sermon/chs218.pdf.

5   Jeremiah Burroughs, *The Wonders of Jesus,* (Crossville, TN: Puritan Publications, 2022) 78.

WEEK FIVE

1   Cambridge Dictionary, s.v. "obey," https://dictionary.cambridge.org/dictionary/english/obey.

2   John MacArthur, *The Gospel According to Jesus* (Grand Rapids: Zondervan, 2008) 37.

3   C. H. Spurgeon, "Solitude, Silence, Submission," (sermon #2468, Metropolitan Tabernacle Pulpit, June 13, 1886), https://www.spurgeongems.org/sermon/chs2468.pdf.

4   Jonathan Dickinson, *The Reasonableness of Christianity* (Crossville, TN: Puritan Publications, 2022) 125.

WEEK SIX

1   Vocabulary.com, s.v. "die," https://www.vocabulary.com/dictionary/die.

2   Dietrich Bonhoeffer, *The Cost of Discipleship* (New York: Touchstone, 1995), 99.

WEEK SEVEN

1   John A. Hardon, *The Question and Answer Catholic Catechism* (New York: Doubleday, 1981), Part 1, Section 4, Kindle.

2   The Sacrament of Penance," Catholic Online, Catholic Encyclopedia, accessed 12/13/2022. https://www.catholic.org/encyclopedia/view.php?id=9131.

3 *Catechism,* par. 1129. This is a restatement of what was originally written in the Catechism of the Council of Trent, 1547, DS 1604.

WEEK EIGHT

1 "How is the Speed of Darkness Faster Than the Speed of Light?," Futurism, August 3, 2014. https://futurism.com/how-is-the-speed-of-darkness-is-faster-than-the-speed-of-light.

2 Spurgeon, "Self-Examination," https://www.spurgeongems.org/sermon/chs218.pdf.

3 Steven J. Lawson, 1 John Overview "Absolute Assurance," podcast audio, August 12, 2021, https://the-bible-study-with-steven-lawson.simplecast.com/episodes/1-john-overview-absolute-assurance-85zq1RZd.

WEEK NINE

1 Cambridge Dictionary, s.v. "reveal," https://dictionary.cambridge.org/dictionary/english/reveal.

2 Dictionary.com, s.v. "convert," https://www.dictionary.com/browse/convert.

3 John Piper, *Future Grace* (Colorado Springs: Multnomah, 2005), 329.

4 J.C. Ryle, "Expository Thoughts on Matthew," https://www.monergism.com/thethreshold/sdg/expository_web.html#matthew.

5 Spurgeon, "Self-Examination," https://www.spurgeongems.org/sermon/chs218.pdf.

6 A. W. Tozer, *The Pursuit of God* (Chicago: Moody Publishers, 2015) 95.

APPENDIX A

1 John Piper, "Command of God: The Obedience of Faith," (sermon, Bethlehem Baptist Church, Minneapolis, MN, Dec. 3, 2006), https://www.desiringgod.org/messages/command-of-god.

APPENDIX B

1 C.H. Spurgeon, "Self-Examination," (sermon 218, Music Hall, Royal Surrey Gardens, Newington, Surrey, London, October 10, 1858), https://www.spurgeongems.org/sermon/chs218.pdf. Small changes have been made for punctuation and accuracy.

APPENDIX C

1 Seven Words, p. 210

Made in the USA
Columbia, SC
15 July 2023

20093170R00102